5
4235

Sweet Sixteen

16 Jazz Duets

For Two Saxes

MUSIC MINUS ONE

MUSIC MINUS ONE

4135
4235

CONTENTS

NOTE: Both alto and tenor saxophone players use the same score on this album. Alto sax players should use the "4135" accompaniment disc, which contains Hal McCusick's performances on alto saxophone, in the correct key. Tenor saxophone players should use the "4235" disc, on which Mr. McCusick performs each piece and part on tenor saxophone in the appropriate key.

ISBN 1-59615-737-2

1. A Swinger

2. A Study in Fragmentation

8 beats (2 measures) precede music.

3. For When Your Wife
Gets Tired Of All That Jazz

4 beats (1 measure) precede music.

4. Back To Dixie

5. Chinatown After Hours

8 beats (2 measures) precede music.

6. For Lovers

4 beats (1 measure) precede music.

♩=92

7. Mood With Variations

*1st Saxophone:16 beats
(8 loud, 8 soft) precede music.*

*2nd Saxophone:8 beats
(2 measures) precede music.*

8. Variations On A Fun Theme

9. Gypsy

4 beats (1 measure) precede music.

10. Harmonic / Rhythmic Study

8 beats (2 measures) precede music.

11. Riff Time

12. Blues, Ballad & Basie

7 beats (1 ¾ measure) precede music.

13. G Swing

8 beats (2 measures) precede music.

14. Torchy

8 beats (2 measures) precede music.

Introduction

POP, BLUES & JAZZ CLASSICS FOR
ALTO SAXOPHONE
FROM MUSIC MINUS ONE

Inspirational

Christmas Memories ....MMO CDG 1203
Various Artists: Have a joyous Yuletide season year-round with this superb collection of seasonal favorites arranged for all vocal or instrumental ranges with orchestral accompaniment. *O Holy Night; O Come, O Come, Emmanuel; Silent Night; Joy to the World; Jingle Bells; O Come, All Ye Faithful; O Little Town of Bethlehem; Hark! The Herald Angels Sing; It Came Upon a Midnight Clear; The Twelve Days of Christmas; Auld Lang Syle*

Pop, Blues & Jazz Classics

2+2=5 *A Study in Odd Times* ....MMO CD 2043
Towson State College Jazz Ensemble/Hank Levy: This collection of stage band classics exploits the unusual meters which became the trademark of composer Hank Levy, whose compositions have been recorded by such greats as Stan Kenton and Don Ellis. *Bop City Revisited; Poopsie's Penthouse; A Quiet Friday; Pete Is a Four-Letter Word; Bread and Watrous; Stillness Runs Deep*

Bluesaxe *Blues for Saxophone, trumpet or clarinet* .... MMO CD 4205
Bob Johnson, tenor saxophone - Eric Kriss, piano & electric piano; **Bob Johnson,** tenor and soprano sax; **Stan Poplin,** acoustic and electric bass; **Jim Chanteloup,** drums: Eight original blues compositions covering a broad range of styles from boogie-woogie to gospel to modern funk, for piano, bass, drums and sax. Listen, then play along. Complete arrangements for both E-flat and B-flat instruments. *Tricky Dicky; When the Spirit; Cocaine Stomp; Wailer Blues; Boogie Breakdown; Tremblin'; Yacey's Fancy; Mad Dog Blues*

Cool Jazz ....MMO CD 4216
Rich Maraday, tenor sax - The MMO Band: Saxophonist Rich Maraday has created an album of originals and contemporary standards for the modern saxophonist, an excellent learning tool for the beginning to the advanced tenor or alto sax player wishing to hone their skills in the genre of smooth jazz. The songs give the player a chance to put his or her personal stamp on the melody as well as on the solo sections. Score includes both B-flat and E-flat parts. *Ribbon in the Sky; Sweetest Taboo; Let it Flow; Saxophone; No Ordinary Love; Unbreak My Heart; All around the World; Another Sad Love Song*

Days of Wine & Roses/Sensual Sax *The Bob Wilber All-Stars* ..... MMO CD 4121
Hal McKusick, alto saxophone - The Bob Wilber All-Stars: Bob Wilber, soprano sax/clarinet; **Hal McCusick, alto sax; Frank Wess,** tenor sax/clarinet/flute; **Joel Kaye,** baritone sax & bass clarinet; **Bernie Leighton,** piano; **George Duvivier,** bass; **Bill Goodwin,** drums: Big-band and jazz legend Bob Wilber brings together a stylish set of classics scored for sax quartet, piano and rhythm section. The four-part voicing, a departure from the traditional big-band era five-man section, makes each voice all the more important and will enhance your pleasure in performing the missing part. *Moon Mist; Days of Wine and Roses; Acapulco Princess; Two Moods for Piano and Winds; The Mighty Hudson; Early Morning Blues*

Easy Jazz Duets *Two Alto Saxophones and Rhythm Section* ....MMO CD 4103
Hal McKusick, alto saxophone - The Benny Goodman Rhythm Section: George Duvivier, bass; **Bobby Donaldson,** drums: This great collection of jazz duets gives you the opportunity to accompany saxophonist Hal McKusick and the Benny Goodman Rhythm Section. Suitable for beginning players, all the selections are great fun. This album allows you to play either duet part. *Farnsworth-Minor The Green Danube; Tone Colors; Reaching Up; Uptown-Downtown; Main Street; Ski Slope; Doing Your Chores; Stop and Go; Glider; Jumper; Da Dit; Hot Fudge; Tijuana; La De Da De; Switcheroo; Swing Easy; Hop Scotch; Swingin' in the Rain; 4/4 Waltz; One Note Break; Lazy; Bits and Pieces*

For Saxes Only *The Bob Wilber All-Stars* ....MMO CD 4104
Bob Wilber, tenor sax; Hilton Jefferson, alto sax: Designed to give the jazz saxophonist (or clarinet or trumpet player) an opportunity to play with a top-flight sax section. Due to the comparative scarcity of big bands today, this is the one area in which young players sorely lack experience. The problems of sight-reading, intonation, phrasing, vibrato, unisons, subtone, etc. which the player will encounter in working with this album are the same one would face playing with a big band. This album should give you an idea of that special thrill one gets when the blend is perfect and everybody's swinging together! Arranged by Bob Wilber. *Countdown; Might as Well Be Movin' On; Waltzing on a Reed; Ballad for Beth; Freemanition; Living for Love; Pork 'n' Beans; Blues for a Matador*

Jazz Standards with Rhythm Section ....MMO CD 3218
Larry Linkin, clarinet: Jazz standards with Larry Linkin as soloist guiding you. Then try them yourself with the rhythm section! *Sweet Georgia Brown; Memories of You; Claire de Lune/Moon River; Oh, Lady Be Good; Porgy and Bess: Summertime; Back Home Again in Indiana; Goodbye; One Note Samba; It Had To Be You; Autumn Leaves; Wolverine Blues; Amazing Grace; Here's that Rainy Day (2 CD Set)*

Jazz Standards with Strings ....MMO CD 3219
Larry Linkin, clarinet: Superb jazz standards with string accompaniments; work your own artistry with this great ensemble! *When Sunny Gets Blue; What'll I Do; That's All; I've Got It Bad and That Ain't Good; In a Sentimental Mood; Our Love Is Here to Stay; Embraceable You; What Are You Doing the Rest of Your Life?; 'Tis Autumn; Night and Day; But Beautiful; Darn That Dream; Ain't Misbehavin'; When I Fall in Love (2 CD Set)*

JOBIM Brazilian Bossa Novas with Strings ....MMO CD 4106
John Sergenian, tenor and alto saxophone - The MMO Orchestra: Join a String Orchestra in these lush backgrounds to the most famous selections in the Jobim bossa nova library. Hear John Sergenian perform them, then try them yourself with the orchestra. *So Danco Samba; Once I Loved; Dindi; How Insensitive; Triste; Quiet Nights of Quiet Stars; Meditation; One Note Samba; The Girl from Ipanema; Wave*

Northern Lights .... MMO CD 2001
Canadian All-Stars Here's the finest band that Canada fielded in 1970 and Music Minus One was fortunate enough to bring them to a studio for these performances from their extensive library. Not to be missed. *Suite Fortune; Dorian Rock Pile; Ballad; Ascendancy; How to Say It; Pete's Thing; My Bones; Get Down! Steve's Theme; Warm; Set-Up Goes Bananas! (2 CD Set)*

Play Lead in a Sax Section *The Bob Wilber All-Stars* .... MMO CD 4120
Hal McKusick, alto saxophone - The Bob Wilber All-Stars: Bob Wilber, soprano sax/clarinet; **Hal McCusick, alto sax; Frank Wess,** tenor sax/clarinet/flute; **Joel Kaye,** baritone sax & bass clarinet; **Bernie Leighton,** piano; **George Duvivier,** bass; **Bill Goodwin,** drums: The legendary Bob Wilber brings you a delectable group of hits scored for saxophone quartet with rhythm section. Wilber himself takes the soprano sax part, Bernie Leighton, George Duvivier and Bill Goodwin back up the saxes. Master alto saxophonist Hal McKusick play the alto part, then you step in and take his place. Play the fully notated version or improvise to your heart's content! *The Look of Love; All Too Soon; No More Blues; Century Plaza; In an Old Deserted Ballroom; A Little Farewell Music*

Sinatra, Sax and Swing .... MMO CD 4217
Brian Hayes, tenor sax - The MMO Orchestra: Australian saxophone wizard Brian Hayes brings you this collection of classic swing standards. A great set that you won't want to miss! *Steppin' Out with My Baby; Let Yourself Go; That's All; (Love Is) The Tender Trap; Oh, Lady Be Good; Fly Me to the Moon; Wave; The Song Is You; I've Got You Under My Skin; Saturday Night (Is the Loneliest Night of the Week)*

Stompin' & Struttin' the New Swing *Six Bands on a Hot Tin Roof* ..MMO CD 4108
In the 20th Century, the year 1998 to be exact, a new swing sound came to our music. Derived in part from the Big Bands of the Forties, and tempered by the music of such jump bands as Louis Prima and Louis Jordan, besides adopting the dress code of the hip-cats of an earlier era (Cab Calloway for instance) these bands played some great music in a more modern, flexible and fun-drenched style. We've taken the most famous songs of these groups, and put them all on an MMO CD for your pleasure and participation. *Hey, Pachuco; The Indigo Swing (style of Indigo Swing); Zip Gun Bop (style of The Royal Crown Review); Put a Lid on It (style of The Squirrel Nut Zippers); Hell (style of The Squirrel Nut Zippers); You and Me and the Bottle Makes Three Tonight (Baby) (style of Big Bad Voodoo Daddy); Zoot Suit Riot (style of The Royal Crown Review); The Ding Dong Daddy of the D-Car Line (style of The Cherry Poppin' Daddies); Jump, Jive & Wail (style of the Brian Setzer Orchestra); This Cat's on a Hot Tin Roof (style of The Brian Setzer Orchestra)*

Studio City ....MMO CD 2021
Cal State Northridge Jazz Ensemble/Joel Leach, Director: Acccompany this exciting, award-winning ensemble! *Ladera Park; Rows of Toes; Dirty Girty; Low Rider; Doin' Basie's Thing; Dancy; Northridge; Dovie; Is There Anything Still there; Big Dipper; The Opener*

Take a Chorus *B-flat/E-flat Instruments* ....MMO CD 7008
Ed Xiques, baritone, tenor, alto and soprano saxophone - Stan Getz, tenor sax; **Hal McKusick,** clarinet & flute; **Jimmy Raney,** guitar; **George Duvivier,** bass; **Ed Shaughnessy,** drums: Designed to give the student player valuable practice in the area of ensemble playing, as well as improvising. Also of interest to the professional who can use it for enjoyment and practice. All ten arrangements have the instrumental parts included with example solos on each tune in smaller notes to serve as a guide. *Fools Rush In; I've Got It Bad and That Ain't Good; Just You, Just Me; How About You?; Sunday; Beta Minus; Jupiter; Spring Is Here; Darn that Dream; This Heart of Mine*

Take One .... MMO CD 2011
Jersey State College Jazz Ensemble/Dick Lowenthal, Director: Dick Lowenthal's prize-winning ensemble, the Jersey State College Jazz Ensemble, is here presented performing the best of their book at the time these were recorded. *Snake Meets the Wizard; Blues for Ross; A Child Is Born; Antithetical Arsis-Thesis; Dancing Men; Nice n' Juicy; She Cries (2CD Set)*

Twelve Classic Jazz Standards *B-flat/E-flat/Bass Clef Parts* ....MMO CD 7010
These historic recordings of standards were made at Judson Hall in Manhattan in 1951 and feature, literally, legends in jazz. Beautiful renditions of some of the finest songs of the 20th century. These backgrounds feature accompaniments by such players as Nat Pierce and Don Abney (piano); Barry Galbraith and Jimmy Raney (guitar); Milt Hinton and Oscar Pettiford (bass); and Osie Johnson and Kenny Clarke (drums). Classic recordings! Includes sheet music for E-flat, B-flat and Bass Clef instruments. The pristine digital transfers of the original recordings put you right there with these jazz immortals! *April in Paris; I Got Rhythm; Oh, Lady Be Good; Embraceable You; Porgy and Bess: The Man I Love; Body and Soul; Poor Butterfly; Three Little Words; What Is This Thing Called Love?; Lover Come Back to Me; I Only Have Eyes for You; Sometimes I'm Happy*

Twelve More Classic Jazz Standards *B-flat/E-flat/Bass Clef Parts* .... MMO CD 7011
This second album of historic recordings continues with a fabulous collection of standards. Your backgrounds for these classics are created by legends Don Abney (piano); Mundell Lowe and Jimmy Raney (guitar); Oscar Pettiford and Wilbur Ware (bass); and Kenny Clarke and Bobby Donaldson (drums). Includes sheet music for E-flat, B-flat and Bass Clef instruments. A true time machine to the greatest days of jazz accompaniments, in digitally remastered sound. *You Go to My Head; Strike Up the Band; I Cover the Waterfront; Too Marvelous for Words; Crazy Rhythm; Don't Take Your Love From Me; Just One of Those Things; My Heart Stood Still; I May Be Wrong (But I Think You're Wonderful) [from the 1929 revue]; When Your Lover Has Gone; Fine and Dandy; Jeepers Creepers*

For our full catalogue of saxophone releases, including more popular and jazz titles, classical concerti, chamber works and master classes visit us on the web at

www.musicminusone.com

Call 1-800 669-7464 in the USA • 914 592-1188 International • Fax: 914 592-2751
email: mmogroup@musicminusone.com

15. Just For Swinging

8 beats (2 measures) precede music.

MMO 4135/4235

16. Triplet Study

Engraving: Wieslaw Novak

Pop, Blues & Jazz Classics for
TENOR SAXOPHONE
FROM MUSIC MINUS ONE

Inspirational

Christmas Memories .... MMO CDG 1203
Various Artists: Have a joyous Yuletide season year-round with this superb collection of seasonal favorites arranged for all vocal or instrumental ranges with orchestral accompaniment. *O Holy Night; O Come, O Come, Emmanuel; Silent Night; Joy to the World; Jingle Bells; O Come, All Ye Faithful; O Little Town of Bethlehem; Hark! The Herald Angels Sing; It Came Upon a Midnight Clear; The Twelve Days of Christmas; Auld Lang Syle*

Pop, Blues & Jazz Classics

2+2=5 *A Study in Odd Times* .... MMO CD 2042
Towson State College Jazz Ensemble/Hank Levy: This collection of stage band classics exploits the unusual meters which became the trademark of composer Hank Levy, whose compositions have been recorded by such greats as Stan Kenton and Don Ellis. An exciting exploration of this now-all-too-rare genre. *Bop City Revisited; Poopsie's Penthouse; A Quiet Friday; Pete Is a Four-Letter Word; Bread and Watrous; Stillness Runs Deep*

Bluesaxe *Blues for Saxophone, trumpet or clarinet* .... MMO CD 4205
Bob Johnson, tenor saxophone - Eric Kriss, piano & electric piano; **Bob Johnson,** tenor and soprano sax; **Stan Poplin,** acoustic and electric bass; **Jim Chanteloup,** drums: Eight original blues compositions covering a broad range of styles from boogie-woogie to gospel to modern funk, for piano, bass, drums and sax. Listen, then play along. Complete arrangements for both E-flat and B-flat instruments. *Tricky Dicky; When the Spirit; Cocaine Stomp; Wailer Blues; Boogie Breakdown; Tremblin'; Yacey's Fancy; Mad Dog Blues*

Cool Jazz .... MMO CD 4216
Rich Maraday, tenor sax - The MMO Band: Saxophonist Rich Maraday has created an album of originals and contemporary standards for the modern saxophonist, an excellent learning tool for the beginning to the advanced tenor or alto sax player wishing to hone their skills in the genre of smooth jazz. The songs give the player a chance to put his or her personal stamp on the melody as well as on the solo sections. Score includes both B-flat and E-flat parts. *Ribbon in the Sky; Sweetest Taboo; Let it Flow; Saxophone; No Ordinary Love; Unbreak My Heart; All around the World; Another Sad Love Song*

Days of Wine & Roses *Sax Section Minus You* .... MMO CD 4210
Frank Wess, tenor sax - Bob Wilber All-Stars: Bob Wilber, soprano sax/clarinet; **Hal McCusick,** alto sax; **Frank Wess,** tenor sax/clarinet/flute; **Joel Kaye,** baritone sax & bass clarinet; **Bernie Leighton,** piano; **George Duvivier,** bass; **Bill Goodwin,** drums: Jazz legend Bob Wilber brings together a stylish set of classics scored for sax quartet, piano and rhythm section. The four-part voicing, a departure from the traditional big-band era five-man section, makes each voice all the more important and will enhance your pleasure in performing the missing part. Clarinetists will find all soprano parts easily playable; Tenor players can play the soprano parts directly with the added bonus of a chance to study the superb soloing. *Moon Mist; Days of Wine and Roses; Acapulco Princess; Two Moods for Piano and Winds; The Mighty Hudson; Early Morning Blues*

For Saxes Only *tenor sax, trumpet or clarinet* .... MMO CD 4204
Bob Wilber, tenor sax; Hilton Jefferson, alto sax - The Bob Wilber All-Stars: Bob Wilber, tenor sax; **Hilton Jefferson, alto sax; Jerome Richardson, alto sax; Seldon Powell, tenor sax; Danny Bank, baritone sax; Dick Wellstood,** piano; **George Duvivier,** bass; **Panama Francis,** drums: Designed to give the jazz saxophonist (or clarinet or trumpet player) an opportunity to play with a top-flight sax section. Due to the comparative scarcity of big bands today, this is the one area in which young players sorely lack experience. The problems of sight-reading, intonation, phrasing, vibrato, unisons, subtone, etc. which the player will encounter in working with this album are the same one would face playing with Ellington, Basie or Goodman. If you haven't had the opportunity to work in a big band, playing with this album should give you an idea of that special thrill one gets when the blend is perfect and everybody's swinging together! *Countdown; Might as Well be Movin' On; Waltzing on a Reed; Ballad for Beth; Freemanition; Living for Love; Pork 'n' Beans; Blues for a Matador*

Jazz Standards with Rhythm Section .... MMO CD 3218
Larry Linkin, clarinet: Jazz standards with Larry Linkin as soloist guiding you. Then try them yourself with the rhythm section! *Sweet Georgia Brown; Memories of You; Claire de Lune/Moon River; Oh, Lady Be Good; Porgy and Bess; Summertime; Back Home Again in Indiana; Goodbye; One Note Samba; It Had To Be You; Autumn Leaves; Wolverine Blues; Amazing Grace; Here's that Rainy Day (2 CD Set)*

Jazz Standards with Strings .... MMO CD 3219
Larry Linkin, clarinet: Superb jazz standards with string accompaniments; work your own artistry with this great ensemble! *When Sunny Gets Blue; What'll I Do; That's All; I've Got It Bad and That Ain't Good; In a Sentimental Mood; Our Love Is Here to Stay; Embraceable You; What Are You Doing the Rest of Your Life?; 'Tis Autumn; Night and Day; But Beautiful; Darn That Dream; Ain't Misbehavin'; When I Fall in Love (2 CD Set)*

JOBIM Brazilian Bossa Novas with Strings .... MMO CDG 4206
John Sergenian, tenor and alto saxophone - **The MMO Orchestra:** Join a string orchestra in these lush backgrounds to the most famous selections in the Jobim bossa nova library. Hear John Sergenian perform them, then try them yourself with the orchestra. *So Danco Samba; Once I Loved; Dindi; One Note Samba; How Insensitive; Triste; Quiet Nights of Quiet Stars; Wave; Meditation; The Girl from Ipanema*

Northern Lights .... MMO CD 2001
Canadian All-Stars Here's the finest band that Canada fielded in 1970 and Music Minus One was fortunate enough to bring them to a studio for these performances from their extensive library. Not to be missed. *Suite Fortune; Dorian Rock Pile; Ballad; Ascendancy; How to Say It; Pete's Thing; My Bones; Get Down! Steve's Theme; Warm; Set-Up Goes Bananas! (2 CD Set)*

Play Lead in a Sax Section .... MMO CD 4209
Hal McKusick, solo alto saxophone - Bob Wilber All-Stars: Bob Wilber, soprano sax/clarinet; **Frank Wess,** tenor sax/clarinet/flute; **Joel Kaye,** baritone sax & bass clarinet; **Bernie Leighton,** piano; **George Duvivier,** bass; **Bill Goodwin,** drums: equel to 'For Saxes Only' offers a series of saxophone quartets (rather than the typical 5-piece arrangement from the big-band era). Hal McKusick provides a complete version to give samples for the improvisational sections, and you have the option of playing the notated solo, or improvising your own. *The Look of Love; All Too Soon; No More Blues; Century Plaza; In an Old Deserted Ballroom; A Little Farewell Music*

Sinatra, Sax and Swing .... MMO CD 4217
Brian Hayes, tenor sax - The MMO Orchestra: Australian saxophone wizard Brian Hayes brings you this collection of classic swing standards. A great set that you won't want to miss! *Steppin' Out with My Baby; Let Yourself Go; That's All; (Love Is) The Tender Trap; Oh, Lady Be Good; Fly Me to the Moon; Wave; The Song Is You; I've Got You Under My Skin; Saturday Night (Is the Loneliest Night of the Week)*

Stompin' & Struttin' the New Swing *Six Bands on a Hot Tin Roof* .... MMO CD 4215
Bob Blank Orchestra & Chorus: In the 20th Century, the year 1998 to be exact, a new swing sound came to our music. Derived in part from the Big Bands of the Forties, and tempered by the music of such jump bands as Louis Prima and Louis Jordan, besides adopting the dress code of the hip-cats of an earlier era (Cab Calloway for instance) these bands played some great music in a more modern, flexible and fun-drenched style. We've taken the most famous songs of these groups, and put them all on an MMO CD for your pleasure and participation. *Hey, Pachuco; The Indigo Swing (style of Indigo Swing); Zip Gun Bop (style of The Royal Crown Review); Put a Lid on It (style of The Squirrel Nut Zippers); Hell (style of The Squirrel Nut Zippers); You and Me and the Bottle Makes Three Tonight (Baby) (style of Big Bad Voodoo Daddy); Zoot Suit Riot (style of The Royal Crown Review); The Ding Dong Daddy of the D-Car Line (style of The Cherry Poppin' Daddies); Jump, Jive & Wail (style of The Brian Setzer Orchestra); This Cat's on a Hot Tin Roof (style of The Brian Setzer Orchestra)*

Studio City .... MMO CD 2021
Cal State Northridge Jazz Ensemble/Joel Leach, Director: Acccompany this exciting, award-winning ensemble! *Ladera Park; Rows of Toes; Dirty Girty; Low Rider; Doin' Basie's Thing; Dancy; Northridge; Dovie; Is There Anything Still there; Big Dipper; The Opener*

Take One .... MMO CD 2011
Jersey State College Jazz Ensemble/Dick Lowenthal, Director: Dick Lowenthal's prize-winning ensemble, the Jersey State College Jazz Ensemble, is here presented performing the best of their book at the time these were recorded. *Snake Meets the Wizard; Blues for Ross; A Child Is Born; Antithetical Arsis-Thesis; Dancing Men; Nice n' Juicy; She Cries (2CD Set)*

Tenor Jazz Jam .... MMO CD 4214
Todd Anderson, tenor saxophone - The Greg Burrows Quintet: Sean Smith, bass; **Kevin Hays,** piano; **Jamie Finegan,** trumpet; **Greg Burrows,** drums: An all-star quintet plays modern jazz charts and invites you to join them in these remarkable arrangements. Not for the timid *Poolside Blues; Summertime; Blue Bossa; Chickory Stick; Night; Serenity; Short Ballad; Revelation (2 CD Set)*

Traditional Jazz Series *Chicago-Style Jam Session* .... MMO CD 4218
Brian Ogilvie, tenor saxophone - Evan Christopher, clarinet and leader; **Jon-Erik Kellso,** trumpet; **Mike Pittsley,** trombone; **Jeff Barnhart,** piano; **Bill Huntington,** guitar; **Jim Singleton,** bass; **Hal Smith,** drums: Emphasizes collectively improvised ensembles and the succession of individual solos in the freewheeling "Chicago-Style" offshoot of New Orleans Jazz., rooted in the swing feel of the late 1930s, with instrumentation typical of the New York groups of this genre. The songs are popular melodies from the 1900s to 1930s as well as multithematic compositions and blues. This album includes both printed solo part and a concert lead sheet, to give you a rare glimpse into the workings of the great bands of the past—and present! Includes a slow-tempo version of the accompaniments to help you get up to speed. *The Darktown Strutters' Ball; That's A Plenty; Rosetta; Poor Butterfly; Sugar (That Sugar Baby o'Mine); 'Deed I Do; Blues (My Naughty Sweetie Gives to Me); The Royal Garden Blues (2 CD Set)*

Traditional Jazz Series: *The Condon Gang*
Adventures in New York & Chicago Jazz .... MMO CD 4219
Anita Thomas, tenor saxophone - **Hal Smith's Rhythmakers: Chris Tyle,** trumpet; **Clint Baker,** trombone; **Ray Skjelbred,** piano; **Katie Cavera,** guitar; **Marty Eggers,** bass; **Hal Smith,** leader and drums: From the 1920s to the 1950s, Eddie Condon and his band created a unique style of traditional jazz, characterized by a succession of instrumental solos and abrupt transitions of dynamics; the result reverberates to this day in the world of jazz. Now you can participate in this incredible style and the sophisticated music of the Condon Gang with this all-digital MMO release. Includes a stellar lineup of professionals giving you guidance and a fabulous ensemble with which to perform! *I Know that You Know; Strut Miss Lizzie; Jazz Me Blues; Skeleton Jangle; Monday Date; The One I Love Belongs to Somebody Else; A Kiss to Build a Dream on; I Must Have that Man; Georgia Grind (2 CD Set)*

Twelve Classic Jazz Standards *B-flat/E-flat/Bass Clef Parts* .... MMO CD 7010
These historic recordings of standards were made at Judson Hall in Manhattan in 1951 and feature, literally, legends in jazz. Beautiful renditions of some of the finest songs of the 20th century. These backgrounds feature accompaniments by such players as Nat Pierce and Don Abney (piano); Barry Galbraith and Jimmy Raney (guitar); Milt Hinton and Oscar Pettiford (bass); and Osie Johnson and Kenny Clarke (drums). Classic recordings! Includes sheet music for E-flat, B-flat and Bass Clef instruments. The pristine digital transfers of the original recordings put you right there with these jazz immortals! *April in Paris; I Got Rhythm; Oh, Lady Be Good; Embraceable You; Porgy and Bess: The Man I Love; Body and Soul; Poor Butterfly; Three Little Words; What Is This Thing Called Love?; Lover Come Back to Me; I Only Have Eyes for You; Sometimes I'm Happy*

Twelve More Classic Jazz Standards *B-flat/E-flat/Bass Clef Parts* .. MMO CD 7011
This second album of historic recordings continues with a fabulous collection of standards. Your backgrounds for these classics are created by legends Don Abney (piano); Mundell Lowe and Jimmy Raney (guitar); Oscar Pettiford and Wilbur Ware (bass); and Kenny Clarke and Bobby Donaldson (drums). Includes sheet music for E-flat, B-flat and Bass Clef instruments. A true time machine to the greatest days of jazz accompaniments, in digitally remastered sound. *You Go to My Head; Strike Up the Band; I Cover the Waterfront; Too Marvelous for Words; My Heart Stood Still; I May Be Wrong (But I Think You're Wonderful) [from the 1929 revue]; When Your Lover Has Gone; Fine and Dandy; Jeepers Creepers*

When Jazz Was Young .... MMO CD 3829
Bob Wilber All Stars: Bob Wilber, clarinet; **Buck Clayton,** trumpet; **Vic Dickenson,** trombone; **Bud Freeman,** tenor sax; **Dick Wellstood,** piano; **Abdul Malik,** bass; **Panama Francis,** drums: One look at the player's list on this album will reveal some of the most famous veterans of the jazz era ('30s through '60s). An opportunity to jam with these jazz giants should not be missed. Under the leadership of Bob Wilber (he scored the film 'Cotton Club'), they present a memorable hour of music-making you'll not soon forget! *Keepin' out of Mischief Now; Chimes Blues; High Society; A Star Is Born: The Man that Got Away; Do You Know What it Means to Miss New Orleans; Tin Roof Blues; Wild Man Blues; Milenberg Joys; Wolverine Blues; When the Saints Go Marchin' in (arr. Bob Wilber); Basin Street Blues*

MUSIC MINUS ONE
50 Executive Boulevard
Elmsford, New York 10523-1325
800-669-7464 (U.S.)/914-592-1188 (International)

www.musicminusone.com
e-mail: mmogroup@musicminusone.com

MMO 4135/4235   Pub. No. 00366   Printed in Canada